$15.00
ISBN 978-1-941550-98-4
spuytenduyvil.net

While we might think that being a speck on a speck is some mere thing, Elizabeth Coleman's poems remind us again and again that each being implicates all others. Here every hip, urban moment is in essential conversation with the past. With a remarkable eye for the finest, most salient details—the way the polished tip of a blind man's cane recalls a mother's painted nails and red lipstick—and a rare poetic ear for recalled and overheard conversation, this poet's newest collection, *The Fifth Generation*, contends with what it means to truly belong, as the concentric rings of our commingled existence ripple outward. This is a book of the most tender intimacies, one in which the speaker reminds us that we are not only members of families but also the bound residents of cities, farms, cultures, histories, and nations, that each of us must finally see as home the whole peaceable kingdom.

Kathleen Graber

# The Fifth Generation

## Elizabeth J. Coleman

SPUYTEN DUYVIL
*New York City*

©2016 Elizabeth J. Coleman
ISBN 978-1-941550-98-4

Library of Congress Cataloging-in-Publication Data

Names: Coleman, Elizabeth J., 1947- author.
Title: The fifth generation : poems / by Elizabeth J. Coleman.
Description: New York City : Spuyten Duyvil, [2016]
Identifiers: LCCN 2015044653 | ISBN 9781941550984 (alk. paper)
Classification: LCC PS3603.O4343 A6 2016 | DDC 811/.6--dc23
LC record available at http://lccn.loc.gov/2015044653

*For my grandparents, parents, children and grandchildren,*
*and for Bob who makes everything possible.*

# CONTENTS

## 1

## 2

## 3

# 4

# 5

# 6

"How extraordinary it is to be here at all."
Stephen Batchelor

1

## FEARLESS

*I want to be a surgeon*, my son announced,
but *since I'm scared of blood,*

*I'll be a blind surgeon.* And I who am scared
to let myself paint, will be a blind painter.

And for fear of mucking up my words, I'll be
a poet without hands. For I am the daughter

of an engineer who was not allowed
to be an engineer, but I no longer know

what is fact and what is myth.
To honor my father, I will not die until

I've painted every New York street, written
an ode to each one, and taken the Circle Line

twenty times around our island, drunk
on cotton candy. The man on the phone

from the Philippines dealing
with my computer crash, keeps saying,

*Now Elizabeth, I want you to remain calm.*
Instead, I think of the acolyte Buddhist monks

sent nightly to the charnel house
to see what awaits us, and I am not afraid.

## Divining

Across from me at LaGuardia, a man and his son
chat quietly.  The young man moves his cane,

tip like a polished fingernail, back
and forth, back and forth.

And I see
your clear polished nails, candy-cane red
                lipstick.

                Everything

reminds me of what
        I want to tell you.

        You'd stand
in the front hallway and pull the curly chord
from the wall,  talk with your cousins:

        Lenore, Esther, Fran—after you'd taken me
to your hairdresser on Riverdale Avenue,

bought me a toy from the store next door, then
a vanilla ice cream cone from Boxer's.  You'd

look up, trim gray skirt, gray hair with its new do.


That final weekend,  when I flew

to see you,  you were skinny the way you'd dreamed.

Hair beginning to grow back, this time not
bushy and full of tipsy enthusiasm.

But  last night you were

      plump again,
      eating steak with butter, your smile,

your lipstick,


          that tiny diastema—

## IMAGINE PEACE

*What are you having for lunch?*
he asked, when I sat down.
*Do you live around here?* No.
*Do you work in this neighborhood?*

The man in the wheelchair wouldn't stop
though I gave one-syllable answers,

       looked away.

*Sid's 95,*

his caretaker said. *Don't tell her that,*
he winked at me, scowled at her.

I tried to ignore him, weary,

       of crowds, heat, subways,
       the chore of getting where

I had to go.


My city can be
like that
       everyone wanting something,

       pigeons pecking at bread.

But then I remembered

the Israeli poet sits beside the Palestinian one
       on my bookshelf,

two men who write of pomegranates,
two languages flowing right to left.

And I remembered the quote
from Philo of Alexandria, a Jew
who lived in Christ's time:

> *Be kind for everyone you meet*
> *is fighting a great battle.*

And so I told the man in the wheelchair,
*I come once a week to play for patients*
*at Memorial,* pointed to my guitar.

*Sid was into music too,*
the caretaker said. *How so?*

I looked up, she with her life before her,
            he trapped in that chair,

me somewhere in between. *Sid's the man*
*who brought the Beatles to New York*, she said.

It was then I saw their twin buttons,
lettering the color of sky, background

the color of light,
            of color without color.

# How Poppies Grow

*for Deborah Warren*

The last time I saw
his silhouette in that red-

stained field of coquelicots,
I was just sixteen or so,

and unfamiliar with regret.

In France they call them

coquelicots, and that day I saw

just how they grow,

in Breton fields at random,
rather than in rows.

## THE FIFTH GENERATION

Grandma showed up last night
in a cream turtleneck and brown
velvet pants. *You look nice,*

I said. *Dressed casually like*
      *that, you look stylish,*
*up to the minute.*

Born two centuries ago,
my grandmother smiled.

If only she'd spoken so I could hear
that thick Russian accent again,
even in a dream.

*People are people,*
she used to say. *What does that mean?*
      my mother'd scoff behind her back.

At the bodega
around the corner, Anna
and the others whose names
I'll never learn now
kept red tins of English Breakfast Tea
for me. They'd call out when I came in,

*Elizabeth,* with a Mongolian accent,
so like song. Last week I went by
for avocados, and to say

hello. *Thank you for last 20 yr*
*lovely Tribeca,* the sign
      on the padlocked door read.

The Gelsey Kirkland School for Ballet,
which spewed out perfect-postured girls

has vanished too, a 60-story luxury building
         springing up
         instead.

Consoled to read of Confederate flags coming down
and rainbow ones taking their place,

I lift my grandchildren to the window
from where they love to watch
construction elevators

                    rise and fall.

## On Trying to Tell My Husband Something Important While He Stares at The New York Times on his I-Pad

Across ancient mountain passes
words gather speed, rip leather
      saddlebags apart,

      scattering:
            kilim rugs,
copper pots, stories to be told,
a mother's paisley shawl.

Sentences fall, crumble,
and the letters blow
      themselves to dust

until only the wind remembers
conversations, the way summer

can mean a hummingbird

yellowy white, alive
but still strange, going by forever.

# A CHURCH FUNERAL

The young woman next to me says she read in the morning paper regulating CO2 will kill the economy. *I just want to learn*, she says, and smiles, teeth like stars. So I tell her of West Virginia's mountain-tops lopped off for coal. From the other side, my son whispers, *The guys from the funeral home look like Mafia in their black suits.* They remind me of Hassidic Jews.

Jews don't embalm our dead to preserve them from decay, but return them to the earth as is. We buried my mother by her parents and brother, my father's ashes scattered to the sea, his name on her gravestone. And Hebrew only on my favorite uncle's grave.

I had a favorite record once, where Yves Montand sang, *She wasted her life, and for what? A lousy mink coat.* My mother had a mink stole. At one end paws; at the other, tiny still eyes. Its softness reminded me of leaning into her as we walked down Fifth Avenue, into Saks, into Lord and Taylor, into the movie theater where we saw *Zorba the Greek*, and the town women wait till Boubalina dies to steal her things. Then Zorba walks into the sea.

*What is it about the sea?* I ask Frances. *We come from it,* she says. I think of the nurse who didn't wait to steal my mother's pearls, and of my fortune-teller who, to do her part, takes pictures of the sun and puts them in the fridge.

# Idyll

The stream sounds like my mother

filling our bathtub,

    porcelain fat-fingered hot and cold handles
quaint even then.

I'm splayed out on grandma's
porch chair, the one
from her apartment patio at 11 Fifth Avenue,
where I watched

    Nixon's impeachment hearings forty years ago.

And while we didn't know
how they'd end,

    things had a way of ending

better then.  I'm scared

of mice, bears, nighttime

silence—not like the city
where someone's always keeping
watch, where I know

    the sounds, sometimes

jarring, sometimes
    smooth,
where smells of pizza, garbage,

mingle with the sea, where mornings
I enter the flowing

crowd. Suddenly everyone's
in navy, or gaucho pants. I hear
Russian, then a language I can't

place.  There's comfort in surprise, in the intimacy
of rudeness. But this loud

blue sky and green of maple
match perfectly. So do
pink dianthus and orange hawkweed,

combinations I wouldn't dream
of wearing in New York where translucent
models  breeze by me on Broadway,
with such confidence and shining hair.

## After Albert Einstein

*I look good, haven't had chemo*
*since December. People survive*
*six years with this one,* I overhear

the woman say, as we sit,
strangers,

    side by side in a restaurant,

molecules intertwined. From there,

a path weaves
    through woods to a lagoon
      where a man, son in tow,

makes skipping stones look
easy, though the physics is precise:
how gravity pulls the stone deeper

    each time, until it can't

escape. The boy tries
to do it just like his dad,

and I wonder again
that you said no to chemo,
    so the hair
you called your shining glory would survive.

## INCOGNITO

Shift done, the conductor glides by,
as a dragonfly scoots from place
    to place, barely lighting down:

*Have a good night: for me, it's Miller time.*

I made a date with the man
I met on a train that terrible year,
then stood him up.  A courteous man
in a clean white shirt, he tried

to reach me several times
by phone.

I'd been living in Paris, where I knew

no one.  There was peace
along with loneliness, strolling through streets,
incognito,  and through the Tuileries,

where girls in smocked dresses reached
for rings from the carousel.  A comfort
in the twang of accordions, whiff

of sweetness from patisseries. Before
the call, unusual back then

        from overseas.  I'd picked up

the black handle unsuspectingly.

Now a different conductor's
coming through with a new refrain:

*New York, New York; it's so nice you gotta*
*say it twice.*

It's always enchanted me
                      how trains start

and stop without the hoopla of planes,
how light softens as the day

ends, like DeKooning's paintings softened
as he aged,  and the ribbons had almost
disappeared.

2

## Saint Simon's Island

A car stops for a loggerhead crossing
a two-lane road to reach the sea. *I doubt
she'll make it*, my son says, *but I'll pretend*

*she did.* Our last day on the island,
we'll try a new spot for brunch and notice
this is the first place we've been
            that doesn't serve turtle soup.

*Maybe it's a sign, ma*, my son will say.

Eisenhower,  the green turtle I bought
at the Ringling Bros.
            and Barnum & Bailey Circus
in '53, died after three weeks.

When I told my mother, she screamed,

*Oh my God,  Nixon is President.*

*Eisenhower has a bad heart, but at least
he has one*, she'd mutter, backing the Olds
out of the garage.

Since ancient times, turtles with their
heart-shaped heads are said to be
the wisest of souls.

By breakfast, mom would have studied
*The Times* as if it all depended on her,
but now she's left gone and left it to us.

## Retreat

On an island where porches are wide as the sea
and palmettos do yoga in the breeze,

where armadillos surprise with bellies of soft fur,
everyone whispered

      she'd had a flesh-eating disease,
arm dangling, ragged, an injured wing.
Her doctor didn't know if it would return.

As our teacher guided us, told us there's more
right with us than wrong, he gazed at the arm
with such tenderness I found myself longing
for him to notice what was broken inside me,

then remembered: I'm one of the fortunate ones.

For I can feel what is no longer there
embraced by what still is—

      *womb, wound, luck,*
all came through low German to me.

## THE GESTATION OF LONELINESS

My husband, in the next room, stirs,
spoon loud against the pot,
and I notice the ticking of the clock
he made by hand.  It's fall;

but we haven't turned
          it back, so it's just getting light.

Soon I'll see the graffiti
on the building across the way, not far
from the apartment, above the Riviera café,
          above the Fortune Society,

where I lost down a bathroom drain
the round coral ring with gold braid
my parents gave me
          when I turned eighteen.

My apartment of being
young and single, and losing
everything, of longing and roommates
and dinner parties, and Tampaxes thrown

loose in a wastebasket, and of Friday nights,
          teaching over for the week,
when I faced two days of seeing
no one but strangers on the street who looked

away, and I thought I was meant
          to be
                    content.

My father loved to quote
        Synge or was it O'Casey:

*If it's a bad thing*

 *to be lonely, it's a worse one*
*to go walking with the fools of the earth.*
Or maybe it was something he made up.

But he knew, my dad: the War
in the jungle, those nine months: the gestation
of his loneliness.

Later I'll read more
        of the letters, paper fragile

as leaves blown
towards my mom.  *I didn't know*

        *one human being*

*could miss another so*, he writes.

He misses his baby daughter too, my older
sister, tried to find her a dress in Manila,

but the sizes were all wrong.

# LOVE SONG

After my argument with the Languedoc innkeeper about
whether to speak French or English—his answering my
French in English, my snapping we'd speak English when
he came to the States—

I returned to our room and opened the door. *Bob*, I called.
And *Bob* again, when no one answered, then walked in
to find a French couple, chic in their nakedness, making
love on the bed against the wall. They didn't seem to
mind me there—the door had been unlocked after all—no,
they were happy to have an audience for a while. It was
obvious, the way they kept at it, rolling around, stroking
the other's perfect body, her round breasts there for me to
see; continuing what they had begun, their mesmerizing
choreography.

At dinner, there was a single candle at the couple's table—
she in skinny jeans and sweater, diamond earrings, he in
black slacks, white shirt—which barely flickered as they
spoke their graceful language to one another. Though I
had loved them more when they were one. And silent.

## OUT OF TIME

*Madama Butterfly* made me nostalgic for gentle snow,
virginity lost in a blue plaid kilt,
before spelling bees were sleek
and slick, when a math teacher could
make you cry, in the days
of a father's old-fashioned glasses
and lop-sided smile. Sundays

were strangely lonely then.  Now
in these woods, it could be any century:
a sunflower with character in its face;
stream slow in late summer as a mother
in a blue Bonnard, drawing a bath,
or a jug of wine poured at a wedding feast.
Butterfly wings like yellow origami.

## What the Sea Wore

Something about the astonishing wind

that day in Belize, where thatched-roofed
wood piers jut into Japanese print blue sea,
and tousled waves cradle
sergeant majors, hogfish, lemon sharks;

> led me to picture
> being born again

in a turquoise shack
by banana trees, frangipani, flamboyants,

into a world where umbrellas are for sun
and not just rain, an old school bus
announces Jesus saves;

where there are four traffic lights, one
at Hawksworth Bridge
> above boats that have capsized in the wind,

and ocean's burlap weave reaches
from sand's tan linen
towards silk sky.

## On Reading *The Invisible Bridge* While Visiting an Old Friend in the Cotswolds

*Please look out the window*, Barbara begs
from the front seat, *look at the ancient*
*hedgerows, thatched roofs, cobbled streets.*

But, I tell her, I don't have time
for wisteria or cyclamen.

Not when I've got to keep Andras and Klara out
of Auschwitz, reunite lovers trapped

in the country my grandfather fled
all those years ago,

where only one in ten Jews will survive.


My parents knew but didn't, like everyone else,

till everything became history, the way

it always does,

and people ask,

*Where were you?*


I want to back up to the last century, be there
when my parents die.

I've read it's not so bad:
that one minute there's life and the next one not.

# Ever After

She slams down the mop: hell, she won't
do another thing for stepsisters

whose only words to her have been
unkind.  And fuck the prince: polished
shoes, slicked-black hair,
                and the pumpkin too.

She's always hated the taste. No, she'll rent
a flat above a shop with a striped awning

in Queens, next to a tobacconist
with its wooden Indian out front,
where she'll sell dresses she has sewn by hand—

brocade and silk, beads of true gems;
every color anyone can dream.

Her store will be open ten to ten.

And evenings when kids play stickball

on the street, she'll lean out,
                greet each of them by name.

# EARLY SUNDAY MORNING

*After Edward Hopper*

Oh the loneliness
of red, of green,
of a street without people,

of my father driving through the Bronx,
us in back holding our breath,
closing our eyes for good luck
as soon as we spotted

the cemeteries.

Later the barber will be in,
all that hair to be shorn.

It falls out in clumps, they say.

My friend told me there's an icepack
her husband insisted on applying himself.
*It never grows back the same*, she said.

With no trees
        on this city block,
you can't tell

if it's hot or cold in Hopper's world,

but the sun shines relentlessly.

        They say when it goes out,
it will be seven and a half minutes

        before we know.

# White Street Synagogue, Rosh Hashanah Eve

Towards the end

of blueberry season, I stroll
for the first time

to a place guarded
by bemused policemen.

Inside, I sit with people

I've never seen before, look

at words set down by bearded men

whose wives ran grocery stores,

and stare at symbols
strange to me.

            We're so few
ephemeral as fleeing clouds on blue.

And I wonder if in the synagogue's minor keys
we hear one thing: the rustle of a book

hidden by a child, in a shtetl, a ghetto
or a hell like Ravensbruck.

## PATAGONIA

The cardiologist from Clearwater
has it right: this land *is* achingly
beautiful, and the wind something
terrible,  Malbec's deep red woven
into the landscape, the depth of color
unexpected.

We're surprised when there are Israelis
on our boat through the rough seas
of the Magellan straits en route to pay

homage to 70,000 penguins

who haven't yet left their private island
for Brazil where they'll escape the winter.

My cousin escaped to Palestine
            when my grandparents came West.

I try to remember what little Hebrew I know.
Finally come up with *boca tov*,
but it's afternoon, and the Israelis laugh.

My grandparents gave Sonia a tractor
before there was an Israel.  And her son Arik
gave me a tiger cowrie shell
for thanks before

            he was killed in the Yom Kippur War.

And I gave it to my cousin named after him,
for his Bar Mitzvah.

                        Like Sonia, these kids
are from Netanya.  One of them knows
her granddaughter.

I want to make it back to Israel before
I die, for even though I don't speak it,
Hebrew is my native tongue.

Or that's how it feels in Patagonia,  where
the penguins love each other for life
and brave the terrible winds.

3

## BUCKET LIST

I write to be surprised,
I told my ob-gyn.  Nor will I
dedicate my life to reading
Proust.

     For that was one man's point of view.

Plus he never left his bed.


I wish I  were a person of many passports
though, like him,

I don't like to travel,

my life
     unraveled the year I was

in France. *Go see your mom,*
*tell her*
*you love her, don't make my mistake,*

     I told my friend.

Mistake, from Middle English
and then back to old Norse *mistaka*

I must remember

to thank my sister for helping me move
that heavy mirror and everything else
out of my apartment
45 years ago when I left for Philadelphia.

I love thinking about my bucket list
and all the places I don't want to go.

From my apartment window, I can see
the water towers, wooden, stolid
            against New York's setting sun.

## In the Farmhouse

Jesus, serene, on the microwave:
Neither he nor my father-in-law have shaved.
Beard, moon-shaped, Amish style, he hunches
over a rough wood cane, clutches rhubarb
in a plastic bag to bring down to a friend at church.

My daughter turns the tape recorder on, and, talking
about old girlfriends, he alludes to the rival
he hit once with a tire-iron. *Grace*, he says,
animated, as if her name came to him somehow,
eyes becoming twenty in that ancient face.

*Knowing she had the TB, she said: please, Roger,*
*go ahead, marry.* My husband, daughter and son
look up, startled, their eyes that glorious
forget-me-not blue that grows riotously on a farm.

# THE PEACEABLE KINGDOM

The boy across the aisle
zips a green spiral
notebook into his backpack,

    frowns with purpose,
a plastic monkey swinging
from his keychain.

In Tanzania, the Masai widows
gave us sweet chai in their only cup
after we helped them save
    rainwater for the dry season.

*Koko* the children called us,
their word for grandmother,
as they watched us dig a trench
into brittle Tanzanian earth.

A guy in a suit fiddles nervously
with a cell-phone, talking
    to another man with a receding hairline.

    They get off suddenly
at 14th. *Don't go*, I want to plead.

*Please tell your friend more about
the unkind thing
your boss said, I want to find out*

*what happened in the end.*

At hotspots, we watched
elegant-tongued giraffes
pull leaves from acacia trees
and blue wildebeest
eat red grasses beside them.

They drank from a common pond
alongside the warthogs whose genus
is their own, strangely graceful
when they're still or kneel to eat,
as if in prayer.

The guy who just got on the train
is carrying an ice-cream maker,
which reminds me of  summer days

in Ohio, sparse clouds, and Bob's mother
        churning iced cream.

Except to say when you were young
an odd uncle's mistake caused

    the fire,

    you hardly said a thing

at all, long-limbed, plaid-shirted,
cowboy-booted, shy.

A stranger in the East,

you told me
of your uncle's wiring error.

How your family stood
        across the road,

and watched the home-place
burn
floor by floor,

    one frigid
December night,  awaiting the fire volunteers.

Tall, cowboy-booted shy,
kindle stronger than desire.

# Getting Past the In-Between

There's a spot along the highway
where Westchester's trees end
and the Bronx's apartment
        buildings begin,

just as sometimes there's a way
        to know
you're changing states,  maybe

a river or tunnel,  but

other times

there's nothing more than a welcome

to Connecticut sign, say,
or to Pennsylvania,

or the wait, quiet,
before snow.

Last night I dreamed
my mother's brother Lewis
        had lived to adulthood,

gotten past the in-between.

My great uncle came first:

*The streets really are paved with gold,*
he wrote from across the sea, and so

the others followed.

## BELIEF

Dick asks if I believe in an afterlife,
and, when I pause, says,
   *Of course you don't.*


But last night I dreamed my two-year old
grandson  was petting Harriet, who died

ten years ago.  *I'm sad you know,*
   he told her,
*I see things,*
   *God, do I see things,*
as he petted her around the face and snout.

And so I went in search of  photographs

   of my four sets of grandparents

at their weddings.

   And placed each
   in a silver frame on the black piano

my mother left me.

And then I put out snapshots
of the eight marriages that came before,

   and the sixteen preceding those, and kept going on and on

until the images stretched
   to eternity,

increasing,  multiplying fruitfully,

back to when we were all the same, to when
we were frogs and amoebas

or the ancient fish they've discovered
that's sensitive to electricity.

## ONE DAY IN A TOWN IN THE SOUTH

through the open
window I heard
the neighbor and her friend,

*That's what you get
for living next door
to Jews,*

she said. A shock
of breeze caressed
my baby's face.

Afternoons I weeded
and drank iced tea     hair

ethnic from humidity

Dogwood blooming
generous as eternity

# Home Movies Were Silent Then

You who nabbed the first seatbelts in New York,
labeled every box and bin, had people come to work
wearing buttons that said,
    *I have a cold,* vacuumed

bees from the porch table, fox-trotted perfectly,
what would you have made of my farmer father-in-law
with manure on his shoes?  Oh, you would have been

entranced by Roger's overalls, missing finger
from a grain elevator accident, the humility.

*I used to play the clarinet,* he said once, then looked
down at his right hand and laughed.  In your way,

in your New York 1950's, fedora at an angle way,
you were humble too. When you learned the man
you'd taught to sail was a famous artist, you scoffed,

*I don't understand modern art,* went back to teaching
him to come about.

You with your size thirteen shoe who sold
your boat the day you mastered tying every knot,

took up the concertina when you heard one
in a Broadway show, followed by an era of bonsai trees.

But that's the thing about death, it's final but not.
You're there in the home movies, thin and happy
in a way I don't remember, like Don on a good day

on *Mad Men.* You're there in photographs, round face,
curvy gray hair, glasses, horn-rimmed on top,
steel on bottom; formal, overdressed for nowadays.

# There's Always a Viper at the Wedding Feast

1.

Only the footsteps, light
as rain, tell him she's there.
Keep dreaming, Orpheus,
you're almost at the top.

2.

She longs more for herself than him,
misses her skin's softness,
how clouds cling to sky.

*I have time to think down here,*
she whispers. *Can you hear me?*
*Can you understand? I would like a life-*
*time with you, but also one without.*

3.

Don't feel shame, Orpheus.
We all dream
        at night of our dead.

        And in the morning
when we turn around, they're gone.

4

# Everyone's Doing the Tango

with its mysterious, afro-Cuban roots,
bandoneonistas, beginnings in working
class neighborhoods, wild rhythm.

The woman at the San Telmo street fair
in a black dress and dancing shoes looks

as if she'll cry.  But she rallies,

and her partner, decked out in fedora,
        vest, and an old pair

of pants you know are the best

he owns, dips her in that melancholy
way my dad twirled my mom
        when they did

the foxtrot.  Funny how debonair

and Buenos Aires have the same root.

And how one dance, one song, can be
joyful, sad
        and angry all at once.

Sometimes I wish you'd bring me flowers,
wild extravagant angels' trumpets and day
lilies with a profusion of smell and white,
the kind you know when they go
bad, you'll catch a whiff of death itself.

## THE DRESS

I was fifteen when Nino Cairone drove me,
convertible top down, from Valdobiadene to Rome.

Small breasts under boat-neck dress—
I wished I was beautifully decked out,

could say the sun-glassed, scarfed things
that would make him lean back,

     breathless, laughing.

My best friend could: bosom, hair tuned up.

But I wasn't foxy enough for this

Marcello Mastroianni sort of man whose wife
financed sleek Italian cars,
long summer lunches on Lake Como.

While I'm sure Nino's forgotten me and all the rest,

I thought for years of the blue-and-white
checks on that cotton, shirt-waisted dress.

## THE MONTH I TOOK TWO PLANE RIDES FROM PARIS TO NEW YORK

*Does daddy have it?*
I asked my sister,
who called from Missouri after dinner
the first night I was back.

*They don't think so*, she said.

*But I guess if the bursitis continues, they'll*

*double-*
*check.*

I've always been grateful for the quiet
way she said it.

On the second trip home,
as the morning light
shone, pink over the wings,
I lied to the Frenchman next to me

who kissed me, a strange lie.

*He's very sick*, I said.

# THE MATH OF IT

1.

It didn't add up:
his white church, my Dutch colonial house;
a father who said tater, had never met a Jew.

I've always been more comfortable with sines,
and easily distracted
by tangents: your sharp angles, home-baked pies,
fascination with fire.

Unbounded sets
measure
love's volume,
a complex number.

2.

Now on the farm a white cat
suns himself
near buildings that had angles
once; falling apart its own

geometry: danger of the wrong

thing said, words a rickety bridge
across a stream, doors

off hinges, trees a startling

green.

# How It Seemed Until Suddenly Everything Changed, or Maybe it Had Been Changing All Along and I Missed It

It was always the same Frenchman in his beret,
shopkeeper with her one black dress,
boy floating a toy sailboat in the park Saturdays.

Year after year, one man, one beret,
white cup holding a café express,
baguette that hardened towards end of day.

He'd always be there in his one beret,
and she in her only fine black dress.

# Marcel Marceau Sous le Pont Mirabeau

*After Apollinaire*

What's the point? Marcel Marceau is gone,
      the great mime here no more.
What will it take to sojourn, stay
open to the pain?

      Urgently now, we learn,
      to let our sons venture more.

Lay me down, let me rest, Sisyphus,
      discuss with you
   the point of nobler pasts, of
eternity's regard, her long silence.

      It's urgent our sons learn,
      that we let them venture more.

A mere send-off becomes an occurrence;
      a mere send-off—
   comely, violet—
becomes different as it evolves,

      and as our sons, ungainly once,
      venture forth.

Passengers, we are past lament,
      night tends to pass away—
   heedless of revenants.
What's the point? Marcel Marceau is gone.

# The Last Digit of Pi

Bisected by a tree, the sun's gold light
draws angles on the glass skin of the pond;
dawn's revellers, a pair of geese in flight
soar high above the wooded hill, beyond
Pythagoras's line of sight. And now
he's all alone, high priest of water, sky,
intuiter of theorems, teller how
this world's the weave of math, the art of Pi.
Another pair of geese approach and glide
across the water, near the grove of trees
he sits beneath. Bird shadows try to hide
amidst the ripples wrinkled by a breeze.
The last of Pi's that stealthy, he decides,
elusive as the wind this dawn light rides.

Lee Slonimsky

## L'Ultime Chiffre

Brisée en deux par un arbre, la lumière
du soleil dessine des angles sur
l'étang ; deux oies se sont envolées
au-dessus de la colline boisée
au-delà de la ligne de mire
du prêtre de l'eau, du ciel, Pythagore,
raconteur de comment l'art de Pi
a tissé le monde, seul, sous un arbre, assis.
Deux oies s'approchent, fendent l'eau en glissant.
Leur ombre joue à se confondre
au milieu des rides d'eau, insaisissable
comme le dernier des chiffres de Pi, pense-t-il,
et le vent monté par la lueur
qu'il contemple, tranquille, au point du jour.

Translation by Elizabeth J. Coleman

# Watching Day and Night

He sees the way a pair of gulls ascends,
as if their destination were the sun;
and wonders what the number two portends,
and if it's twice, or vastly more, than one.

Much later he spies geese that move as three,
their feathered arrow floating toward the west,
and wonders what significance could be
in triangles, as night delivers rest.

Four willows weep along the old stone fence
on which he sits, the sky pure darkness now;
he longs to make a perfect, mystic sense
of all the numbers earth and mind allow.

Perhaps dividing thirteen into seven
lies just beyond the starsplit door to heaven.


Lee Slonimsky

## GUETTER, JOUR ET NUIT

Il voit deux mouettes s'élancer si haut
que leur but parait être le soleil
et se demande ce que le chiffre deux présage,
s'il est deux ou plusieurs fois plus qu'un.

Plus tard il observe des oies voyager à trois,
une flèche de plumes flottant vers l'Ouest ;
et se demande ce que les triangles signifient,
alors qu'arrive le repos de la nuit.

Quatre saules pleurent le long d'un vieux mur de pierre
où il s'assied; le ciel est d'un noir pur.
Il tient à comprendre le sens mystique et parfait
de tous les nombres sur la terre et dans sa tête.

Peut-être qu'au-delà de la porte du ciel,
on divise sept par treize au milieu des étoiles.


Translation by Elizabeth J. Coleman

5

## LOVE POEM

When F. Murray Abraham, son
of a Syrian Coptic Christian

who was playing Shylock, came out
for his curtain call, he picked up

the kippah Portia had thrown down,
kissed it and put it on his head,

before he took his final bow.

And I thought of how

during my daughter's green hair phase,
she scolded: *don't you dare dye yours,*
*let it grow gray gracefully.*

And of how when I was little, I'd lean into
my mother for a moment in the back seat
of the car and she into me, right before

we left for the shore, where
my father would take us sailing,

white cap cocked to one side,
the image of a life

preserver entwined with a rope embroidered on.

I thought
of my daughter's twins

and their tiny hands.

Since the morning the towers fell,
I say I love you promiscuously.

I've noticed it in others too.

When I was leaving the restaurant next door
the other day, I said it to our waitress

by mistake, it just slipped out.

# THE OLD NEIGHBORHOOD

Down the hill beyond the rocks
the glaciers brought eons ago,

the Episcopal Church where I took
dance lessons, wore white gloves, and thought

only I

had never kissed a boy

                    looks tiny now.

At the bottom of the other hill
was the Conservative Synagogue.

Sometimes I'd go with the neighbors
to the ancient yellow building
that would one day burn down,
listen to the old men drone on

in Hebrew. Or I'd go next door
for dinner Friday night,
watch them light the candles.

How fitting we lived in between:

my father raised Episcopalian,
my mother born a Jew.

And I loved it all: the Christmas
Carols my mother called American
folks songs, the Hebrew prayers
I couldn't understand, and that we were
somehow everything, and nothing
all at once.

Two-toned yellow honeysuckle
climbed between the neighbors' house and ours,
above the black asphalt driveway
I assumed would be there always.

If you broke off the tip
in between, where the flower comes
from the stem, there was a quick taste

of sweetness.

# THE HOMELESS CAT WHO FOUND US YEARS AGO MAKES A CAMEO APPEARANCE IN MY DREAM

In the fur-soft morning sky, Chloe appeared
by the garage one day, genteel as a widowed
aunt who's come to stay

                 in a lilac-printed dress,

and she trotted gamely through our mess.

While the dogs barked, and children hurled
their food, Chloe lapped her milk, as in bed

the night before tongue had met lip, that first
steady sip. Now here she is, miniature tiger
wandering through the jungle of our lives, stuff

strewn, my high heels, your patterned ties.

For a moment, that house on the hill behind
the giant magnolia tree is ours again;

tables finally dusted, shoes in the right bin,

everything right,

  just before the guests come.

# THE COLOR OF HAIR

I'd finally gotten up the nerve

to fire the guy who for fifteen years
stared at French TV news

while he cut my hair.

He glanced at it once towards the end

to suggest highlights.


But my mother's hair had been gray,
my grandmother's too.

And now I could rebel by not rebelling.


Against Clairol, and everyone who ever

called a woman of a certain age a hag
or crone.


                    I'd seen a play about Carol King

and how slowly she'd stopped setting her hair, and
dying it.  Instead, she'd let it grow gray,

                        now kept its natural curl.

She was singing her own songs

rather than covers, and no longer put up

with her husband's fooling around.

The other day, I was quizzing

my grandson on the color of things
at the restaurant table.  After

I ran out of cups and saucers and napkins,

I asked, What color is my hair?


He seemed stumped at first,

But then, knowing he was about
to nail it,  he smiled.

Silver, he said.

## Remembering my Christmas Eve Visit to a Friend In the ICU Three Days Before She Died, and What Had Come Only Weeks Before

I was waiting for her in a restaurant
on Central Park South when a woman
ran across the street, against the light,
and I thought: who is that sexy older,
woman in the low-cut turquoise dress?

She pulled the wooden chair out
from the plastic table with a flourish.
*I bought it on the street, in six colors,*
she announced, triumphant.

# THE MAN WITH THE RED SCARF

*Is that your New York Times?*
the man on the A Train asks.
He's wearing a red scarf, tied
in a Parisian knot.

*The paper costs $2.25 now,*
        *but it's hard times,* he says,

        then pauses.

*I'm reading*
*yesterday's front section carefully,*
*with its important information.*

*You could go to the library and read*
*it there,* I suggest in my helpful voice.

That afternoon, a cellist in black tie
will play Bach's Sixth Suite
on the Highline Trail.

                Smiling tourists
will ask me to take their picture with him,
and I'll think of the man on the train.

*I'd love to,* I'll tell them.

A woman outside a café will
hand out red balloons.

But soon I'll return to my bad habits

until I'm reminded again

after the San Bernadino shootings,

and buy a banana nut muffin
and a regular coffee for the woman
who sits under a white blanket
on West Broadway.

As I lean in to hand her the muffin,
she'll flash me a smile. I'll notice
the freckles around her eyes
and wonder who I am

to decide what kind of muffin she likes,
and how she takes her coffee.

## WINTER BLOOMS

The Catskills loom, alluring in a Sleepy
Hollow sort of way, folding over
one another like laundry, back when

people had time to fold, winter days
were cold, and weather wasn't a sport
of nature.  But flowers bloom in winter

now: daisies and daffodils, forget-me-
nots and, famously, cherry trees.
It will be said there was a time

old women rinsed their hair in blue,
good news came by mail, bats were plentiful,
and you could walk to Newark on the ice.

I tell the super who's cleaning our air
conditioning vents I'm uptight
about all this warm weather in winter.

                    He's pleased
about the lower heating bills, he says,
how great it feels to go outside.

*Wouldn't it be nice if we could choose
the weather?* Jimmy adds. *But,* I ask him,
*who among us would decide?*

6

# One Way of Looking at Grace

For 150 million years birds saw
their reflections only in the sea,

but now the last typewriter repair
shop in New York is going out

of business, and monk parrots
nest in Sheepshead Bay.  Still

that fire escape casts a lovely shadow,
the way the wheel of a slow-moving

bicycle seems to slow time,
gorillas stay up all night to groom
their dead,  and a woman in Ohio

who's been laid off is giving every building
in town a new coat of paint.

*What's your name?* I ask the woman
at the post office who always takes my packages
and tells me about her cruises
to the Bahamas with her mother and sister,

and how much they love
the all-you-can-eat buffet.

*Grace*, she says, *I thought you knew.*

# THE DIRECTION

I scour the paper for good news
after last night's dream where
death was a terrible speeding
up rather than a slowing down.

Bob grabbed my hair but
we couldn't hang on to one
another, and floated apart,

unmoored. I wonder what
she dreams all these years later,
the woman whose son went off

to catch the school bus that morning.

They say she spends afternoons
on her fire escape smoking and looking
in the direction he went.

## The Cyclopes: I Serenade the Moon

I wake to find you spying
on my dreams,   one-

eyed giant,

solipsistic shape-shifter,

disembodied  flashlight

prying curtains open.


      I brace myself

for the interrogation.


You follow me
            to another room,

where, by your light,

Cyclops woman, my guitar—

      small-breasted,
      big-hipped—


belts out her song.

# Meditation on a Chaise Longue
## at Hudson River Park, Lower Manhattan

There are no landmarks any more except that
lovely Lackawanna sign

*May you be happy  people on the tug*
*May you be happy two little trees*
*and five more I see from the shore*

I miss the old piers  the Hudson no longer smells like the sea and
I miss the Palisades     the rollercoaster I wasn't scared to ride

I want to cover myself with tattoos like the woman running by

There's Ellis Island and the Statue of Liberty   what
my grandparents first saw
more than 100 years ago

*May you be happy    people on the Circle Line*
                          *as you circumnavigate New York*

I love the way boats ply the river nice and slow
There's a small American flag above
the Lincoln Tunnel   understated    jaunty

Where are all the seagulls?
Did they create that seductive smell of death?
Yet people say there are still gulls

The sun—a flower — shines on a tall glass building
and reflects back into the river as if moonlight

Seven ducks on the river   white bottoms   floating
like little people in a miniature pool
holding mixed drinks with tiny paper Chinese umbrellas

The ducks clean their feathers   dive   ride the waves
wood-ducks floating on the Hudson quiet     content

Do they know they're in the greatest city in the world?

And there's a little boy running and his older brother and their mom
*May you appreciate their good health   mother of two boys*

## Our Garden in Summer

There are moments when I think
I'll never feel

    despair again:

a laugh, a glass of wine,
lunch with a friend, opening
a present one of the children

sent. I'm always surprised
to witness its return.

Sometimes halfway through

the night, I catch

    a glimpse

of the abyss my parents, grandparents

slipped into; other people I forget

to miss. And wonder how many more

white cone-shaped hydrangea blossoms

I'll see on that tree you

planted that's grown tall on our hill

by the cabin
    nestled in the Catskills Park,

outside Phoenicia, beyond
Big Indian, past Oliverea, not
far from the road to Frost Valley

after you turn right—

## SONG OF INNOCENCE

In our family we never put the milk bottle
on the dining room table, placed the napkins
—cloth—in our laps.

We played the black baby grand,

had fresh red and white asters

in the front hall, gave children
the names
        of kings and queens, and said

    *how do you do*

to strangers.  And there was no
TV in the living room

except that one day, when my parents
moved it into the dining room
while we ate lunch, and we saw

Ruby shoot Oswald live

    in black and white.

Right before one o'clock French class,
the day before, Mr. Heller had straightened
the pictures on his wall,

and, like they always did
the boys had made them crooked again.

## Patatakan Farmers Market

The guy who sells vegetables at the first stand,
Richard, wears his hair the same length as his wife
who has a little nose-ring on the side—a different

    one each week.  Today

it is a star.  My cousin,

a watch wholesaler, says Richard would be perfect
in a jewelry ad, warm smile, shoulder-length hair.

I think: what,

nice people, when

out of the blue, a blue like the great bright sky

today above the market,  I picture them walking

across a field, then see them

    shot,

like in the film where the farmer hides

the Jews

under the floorboards, and has to choose
between them

and his family.

Richard has a tan
from working in the sun. Their crops
ruined

in the flood this spring,

Customers took up a collection.
*Lucky Dog*, they call the farm.

## ROMANCING TAXIS

I step outside, call out to one
hail it, beautiful sunflower.

My grandchildren love
the sunshiny color too,

the optimism in the bold
way cabs announce their presence,

pull over cockily
to the curb,

let you know wordlessly

I'm here and I'm going to pick you
up, just you,

and take you
wherever you need to go.

They were my saviors when I was young
and alone and New York was mean,

and I was careless of myself.

# When There's No Itinerary

*After Hurricane Irene*

In the night the stream becomes a river

that makes our grove disappear,
maroons us on a tiny spit of land—

no food, water, lights, phone.

Bob says we're stranded

like on *Lost,*
        but I could never bear to watch,

need to know

                how the story ends.

On the open fire he makes me
cowboy coffee.

        That's what our guide called it anyway
that summer we floated in dories down the Colorado,
like John Wesley Powell the year he mapped the territory.

We too slept along the shore wherever we happened

to light.

        In a startling red top and braids pinned

to her head, a style she'd never worn before,

our daughter

squinted at the sun, paddling  her kayak alongside us.

And our son,

wearing his blue and white striped sailor shirt,

floated valiantly in a boatful of strangers

       towards the chaos of Lava Falls.


The neighbors' house has been made to vanish too,
leaving nothing


except a hand-painted wooden sign that reads:

*Maple Syrup Sold Here.*

# CHUTZPAH: EARLY EVENING, BROOKLYN HEIGHTS

My daughter tells me she heard
a scientist on the radio describe
the first photos from Jupiter.

*He said it made him realize*
*we're just a speck on a speck,*

*and I was oddly comforted,*
she told me.  As I am at dusk

when the chutzpah of Manhattan's

skyline appears. Tonight's full moon

smaller than the street-lamps,
smaller than that lit-up Audi.

ACKNOWLEDGMENTS

I would like to thank the editors and publishers of the following publications where some of the poems in this volume have appeared or will appear:

*Let My Ears Be Open*, Georgetown: Finishing Line Press, 2013: An earlier version of "After Albert Einstein" as "Weekend in Maine;" an earlier version of "A Church Funeral" as "What Is it About the Sea?;" and an earlier version of "How It Seemed…" as "Morning."
*Per Contra*: "Divining," "How Poppies Grow," "Idyll," as " What Began as an Ode to a Cabin in the Catskills," "One Way of Looking at Grace," "There's Always a Viper at the Wedding Feast," "Romancing Taxis," "Two Decades in the South."
*The Saint of Lost Things.* Santa Rosa: Word Temple Press, 2009: an earlier version of "White Street Synagogue" as "Towards the End;" an earlier version of "Out of Time" as "In these Woods."
*Pythagore, amoureux/Pythagoras in Love,* Meredith: Folded Word, 2015 © 2007, Lee Slonimsky, © 2015 Translation copyright, Elizabeth J. Coleman: "The Last Digit of Pi"/ "L'Ultime Chiffre" and "Watching Day and Night/Guetter, Jour et Nuit." *Pythagoras in Love* was originally published by Orchises Press in 2007.

Additionally, I want to extend heartfelt thanks to my poetry teachers: Mark Cox, Emily Fragos, Richard Jackson, Thomas Lux, Marie Ponsot, Natasha Sajé, Betsy Sholl, Lee Slonimsky, Estha Weiner; and to thank poetry colleagues who gave me invaluable feedback on these poems: Kate Fetherston, Susannah Laurence, Sonja Haussman Smith, Fiona Sze-Lorrain. Many thanks, too, to Lucy Jane Stroup for her wonderful advice on my cover art, and to Laurence Magro for her consultations on the French translations.

I also want to thank those who have helped me so invaluably on this journey: Rob Casper, J.S. Graustein, the late Daniel Hoffman, Sharon Israel, Miriam Kotzin, Brett Fisher Lauer, Anne Marie Macari, Alice Quinn, Michael Salcman, the late William J. Smith, Gerald Stern, Deborah Warren, the Powow River Poets, and many others.

Finally, I want to thank the poet Kathleen Graber for her brilliant and generous guidance in working on this manuscript, and all my friends, teachers and colleagues at the Vermont College of Fine Arts for their support and friendship over the years.

ELIZABETH J. COLEMAN is the author of *Proof*, a poetry collection (Spuyten Duyvil Press, 2014), a finalist for the University of Wisconsin Press' Brittingham and Pollak prizes. She has also written *Let My Ears Be Open* (Finishing Line Press, 2013) and *The Saint of Lost Things* (Word Temple Press, 2009), two chapbooks of poems. Elizabeth is the translator into French of poet Lee Slonimsky's *Pythagoras in Love* (Folded Word Press, 2015). Elizabeth's poetry has been published in numerous journals, and her poems appear in *The Bloomsbury Anthology of Contemporary Jewish American Poetry* (2013), and *Poetry in Medicine Anthology* (Persea Books 2014). Elizabeth is also an attorney. She can be visited on the Web at www. elizabethjcoleman.com.

29304682R00069

Made in the USA
Middletown, DE
14 February 2016